Dmitri's Agenda

by
Malcolm McCollum

YouArePerfectPress

"Baseball" published in The Mississippi Review, Spring, 2003
"Just Say No" published in Colorado Springs Independent, May, 2004
"Dmitri's Agenda" published in Toiletpaper 4, March 2005

Copyright © 2016 Malcolm Stiles McCollum
All rights reserved

ISBN: 978-0-9844139-3-5

Library of Congress Control Number: 2016932156

YouArePerfectPress, Lancaster, NH

For Virginia Stiles McCollum and Helen Stiles Chenoweth, Yevgeny Yevtushenko, Peter DeLissovoy, and for all my friends: Semper Fi

Forward

Dmitri Ashkanov first crossed my path in the early 1990s at Nelson's Books where he worked as a clerk. For a couple of years, we spent a fair amount of time together, in the bookstore and in the taverns and coffee shops down around van Buren. Dmitri didn't bother with personal resumes when he met a new person. He just started talking about something other than himself. I enjoyed that characteristic, and enjoyed the melodies and rhythms of his voice, and the odd things he noticed. At some point, he gave me permission to record him when we were having a drink or ten and he was rolling. These are the transcripts I've culled from hours of tape.

Dmitri just disappeared one day without leave, without a trace. Not even Harry at Nelson's Books knew where he'd gone or why. If he'd fallen victim to one of the city's victimizers, his body never turned up, so far as I knew. I prefer to hope that he just felt it was time to cross some other paths on some other streets than Chicago's.

Magic

> All knowledge is awakening to larger dimensions of what is unknown.
> - I Ching: Shih Ho

Long ago, when Johnny Carson young,
Dmitri see machine on show,
plain, black box length of inventor arm,
one silver button on top corner of long side.
When inventor push button,
lid slowly lift, as top of coffin, and from it emerge
one white-glovèd hand with index pointing,
rise up on mechanical arm,
pause, pivot, descend
to poke button which set it free,
ascend, pivot, pause
and then retreat beneath closing lid.

Remember Dmitri tell you this,
while he tell you something else.
Dmitri don't know.
You don't either.

Unseasonable Happy

At lunch today, took stroll in Grant Park,
in rain so gentle nearly hover,
coat open to almost warm that now
for three days bless this February.

Much dirty snow have percolated
into ground, revealing umber shingles
leaves and flatted grass already
perking, like boy hair in bed at dawn.

And what rich smell of life rise
from all this rotted brown and
crushèd, bleachèd straw, soften
by snow, revealèd by rain,

watch over by bare, black branches
in soft grey air. Pass by
Art Institute lion on way back to store.
Roar back at them.

Aaron Neville

Sitting in tavern on South Wabash,
look up, see on television set one very,
very ugly man, black man with great growth
on forehead, huge shoulder, neck.
Think, another show about black criminal
everyone fear here.

No. Grotesque black giant open mouth and
Dmitri expect curse, but instead sing.
With voice that angel if were any
would put head under wing for shame
and envy, with voice that say "Look, look
at beauty of this world and never mind angel."

Voice transport Dmitri back to Amsterdam, where
once visit former lover, sad story that,
now live over canal with rich Dutch man.
We are making talk together, and Dutch lover man
bring out book, open it. Look, Dmitri, he say,
what you think of these fellows here?

Look. Photo of some guys standing in front
of farmhouse-looking hovel, straw and black mud,
look like they grew up out of mud, dirty,
low muddy hair over low muddy brow,
like first man. They just stand looking back
at camera as if wish to kill owner.

Look more, knowing this now lover testing
former lover, Dmitri. Late weak sun
through film of drapes, watery light like pearl.
Think, I hope I don't ever get left alone with
these guys in picture. But say
words in Russian, as if can't put thought into word

host enemy can understand. Then,
like coward, say, "These men look formidable ."
Surprise: my host enemy find this passes test.
These men, he say, are Frieslanders , and
took three hundred and more Jews away from Nazis in
little boats over sea to England.

Think about this as Aaron Neville on TV
in Chicago tavern sing, about these men
no one would welcome if walk in here,
maybe anywhere, who yet put lives onto sea
time and time, night and night, for people
maybe they even hate, but save from murder.

Best, still, Dmitri like to hear Aaron Neville
sing song Mona Lisa .

Harry

All who know his shop call him Harry,
though shop called "Nelson's Books."
Dmitri call own boss Harry,
only because he ask to do so.

Not mathematician, Dmitri have counted
hairs left on Harry's head
so many time that sure: three left,
very long, most carefully arrangéd

in halo formation, and quite right so,
for Harry saint of book if ever was.
And in old age, like Zen priest,
Harry out of patience with almost all

but those who share love.
Need clerk, like Dmitri, who care
for no one, nothing, only, like Harry,
for truth, like Dmitri, for live soul.

This morning, Harry say "Morning."
Behind rimless eyeglass, dark pouch.
"Morning," Dmitri respond, think,
hope you not die yet, old man.

If die, who left to believe that word
on page in black print matter,
who left to love reader,
who left to run this store?

Dmitri Do Not Dance

Dmitri think much about women in these days.
Read what they ask for in personal advertisement.
Always, say "like to dance, like long walk, quiet time,
Romantic evening by firelight," etcetera, etcetera.

This correspond not with any real woman Dmitri have
had mixed pleasure to know. Real woman, once trap
has snappèd, have no time for long walk or even short,
and quiet time by firelight mean Dmitri, shut up

while I burn you with mouth. Make nice glow, you.
One exception is dance, which all woman truly like,
though many different thing mean by that, from do step
as in book to weave about ignoring music entire.

Dmitri do not dance. Dmitri hear music too much
to find way to move to except alone, and do not like
step from book, as in example waltz,
one-two-three and on so for many minute over.

Watch trees dance with wind. Some time trees
all dance together, bending tops in one direction
in arch like ballerina's arms while trunk unmovèd.
Bend with wind, all leaves upturn and silver.

When wind too much for dancing, trees break,
big branches split and crash down to become dead.
Nobody perfect. Nobody live forever. Dmitri
do not dance. Dmitri dance all the time.

Beautiful Girl

Walking up Western Avenue, Dmitri see this:
In front of apartment, beneath young elm green,
girl in white dress whirling and whirling,
someone, her father surely, taking picture.

Under shade of elm and building,
she appear like flower upside down,
gown whiter than lily, head black.
Behind her, green window sashes.

She whirl and whirl, dad shoot, shoot.
Limousine pull up to deposit boyfriend
To take daughter away. They go.
I watch dad die on way up walk to house.

He know well what life hold ready to give her,
roll of nickel in glovèd hand boyfriend hold
out to lead her into limousine. And envy
her not to know. And go back into house.

Progress

In old time in Wabash Street tavern,
was silent as Sorrow's nephew drowning,
bubbles rising through glasses along long bar.
Chair might shift, wood scrape on wood,
cash register once in while go dja-tinngg as
car go by in street outside, or alley.

Now, over bar, three TV screen launch
salvo after salvo stuttering flash,
cannèd so-call music scream and pound,
no one cannot talk no more, nor
peaceful drown, nor could hear tank go by
in street. Or stop and wheel at door.

Message

Dmitri love commercial. Especially
love they are called "message" -
worthy of Pravda genius, that word.
Here is best one yet. First see old man,

maybe age of Dmitri, but not so handsome,
few strings rat gray hair, days of dirty silver stubble,
sick rodent eyes behind thick glasses.
To complete picture, only missing t-shirt saying

"Pederast and Proud Of It." Girl approach
this vile creature. She has usual these days
metal rings hanging from face parts,
black, not-washèd hair, lipstick color dry blood.

"Do you have something I like to read?" she say.
"What like?" inquire pederast. "Have Homer's Odyssey
in original Greek?" she ask, and pederast quick reply,
"Attic, Doric or Ionic?"

Girl drop jaw to indicate condition stunnèd, say
"How is that possible?" "I have every book
in every language in every edition ever publish,"
say nasty geezer with smug mouth.

Then some logo for some digital thing appear, and
voice say something about company.
Like many message, this leave Dmitri in dark
what he suppose to buy. Not Homer, surely.

But of course Dmitri get real message clear and loud.

Is Information Age. All knowledge instantly
available - oh, sound most heavenly choir of angel,
for we are savèd. All is known.

No crock big enough yet fashion for such idea.
This dull-eyed, dirty girl, she would not comprehend
Odyssey in any language, for even Homer say
that even smartest man
must travel far, pay much to understand.

Dedushka

Some guys Dmitri meet at Wrigley Field,
all drunk to watch Cubs blow yet another lead,
later in week take Dmitri fish
for lake trout. One own boat, one rod and reel

to loan, and on that rod and reel Dmitri
hook something big, make rod tip plunge.
Set hook. Hoist, reel in. Hoist, reel in.
No fight, no life. Big can of lard, Dmitri

think, but no- when fish at last emerge,
is trout, but trout like Hieronymus Bosch would catch,
moldy white except for brown flower
warts. Fish very, very next to dead.

Revolting. Wrigley brothers laugh - fish
remind of Cubs, dead though appear alive.
Dmitri laugh, but at comparison,
not at his trout, trout that to live must eat,

trout that to eat must live, though dying,
long enough to drive up from black bottom
of Lake Michigan and take Dmitri bait.
Scrofulous, sick, repulsive as might be,

this fish die trying yet to live.
Sought only for pleasure human acquisition,
despisèd for how life has disfigurèd,
fight to his end, though can no longer fight.

Voices around him loud and laughing beer,
Dmitri look over grey roll of shoreless lake
and seeing unseen shore,
think, if anything holy, is this poor fish.

Just Say No

When Mrs. President offer brilliant idea,
"Just say no to drug," seem perfect.
American people love simple above all else,
except to say No. No, no, child; no, no.

If Mr. President not on drug, how could say
"No poor people in America?" Yet he say this.
Yeltsin frequent drunk, yet even he see poor.
American President drug must stronger be.

Biggest drug, Dmitri think, to be Right.
If right, then one can sit on can,
despise all, love nobody, feel good.
Dmitri just say no to Right.

Also to Be Good All Time.
To seek this, man must become other
than man, and then monster.
Dmitri may testify to this; was monster once.

Dmitri drink far too much and often.
Hurt him, hurt other, sometime.
Drink to keep from good all time,
like pretty woman who only say No.

Jay McShann

All great pianist have great time,
know as precise as great fisherman
exactly where beat or bait
must go. Only greatest hear
no beat but one that universe make.

Great fisherman know where fish
lie or swim beneath plash and shine
of little wave, invisible in dark
but there. But alive. There and
not there. So lie and swim beat.

Of all pianist Dmitri ever hear,
none have understood beat
like Jay McShann. Touch piano key
as fisherman touch line on reel
when cast, with infinite attention.

And know as fisherman know
that all is circle, and control is
riding circle. That is swing.
That is fishing. Beat is circle,
as Charles Mingus say.

Dmitri once see McShann alive
at concert. While listen, watch face.
Look like relief map of old country,
volcano weatherèd by time to hill,
river full mysterious fish, smile in sun.

Baseball

Baseball American poem about life,
say many, and Dmitri think true.
Very greatest hitter, Ty Cobb, fail 6 of 10 times,
very greatest pitcher maybe succeed that much.
Great fielder may go many, many play
without error, but one day easy ground ball
look like Krazy Kat cartoon to him,
and there before his thousands fans
he step all over own dick. Life.

Young genius of diamond frequent appear,
he cannot containèd be in April, May -
but then old men around league,
they have watch, remember all see,
and in July, when grass grow slower,
old men have talk and genius sudden
cannot buy hit, cannot throw strike three,
start throwing ball in own dugout.
Then nothing look anymore so green.

Also, not strong, not fast, not anything
but try harder than gifted ones
may have place on baseball team. This happen
every day, but Dmitri never forget World
Series 1960, first one for him in this new country.
When all seem lost for Pittsburgh Pirates,
bad hop make Kubek err, then Mazeroski
end everything, homer in 9th.
He never almost hit homer before or after.

Also, most gifted player may be poison man,
and so may poison whole team. Dmitri name
no name, for who can truly judge who is not part
of team, but yet Dmitri has seen great star
come down in dugout from home run trot,
how some players sudden thirst for water,
others go to bat rack, though far from next up,
others develop interest in crotch,
all avoiding the obligement of "high five."

And how one player, never mention by
sporting scribe, may hold whole fate of team
in hand. One year, team may have great leadoff
man, know how to get on base and fast enough
opposing pitcher must think of him. Each batter
after become better. Divided mind of pitcher
guarantee that. But then leadoff man slump;
whole team slump, and great cleanup man
cannot hit shit with canoe paddle at noon.

And what does cause great leadoff's slump?
Oh God of Base Ball, who could count such cause?
Wife gone cold, wife delivering child,
Bonus foolish lost, wrong step on stair,
wrong word said at right time,
right word said at wrong, inch of front foot
left or right in box, bad dream recallèd
by good song, good wine, bad wine,
no wine. Oh who could count the cause?

In this country, people think athlete stupid.
Here is stupid: with man on first, hard grounder hit
to hole which shortstop barely stop, backhanded;
he pivot, fire to second, where second baseman
has one tenth second to catch, touch bag, know
character of runner coming in, decide how hit his
base, throw body out of way, know where body is
in space at exact moment he release throw to first
from no ground to stand on. Make perfect throw.

Know self, say Socrates. That second baseman
know self like no Greek talker ever did.
As did Hawk, great Andre Dawson, know
not only self but all opposing pitcher, due to
study, study, study of own book he write
every day, and so stand ready for anything
anybody have to throw, poisèd like great
Zen archer to answer question before put.
Uncoil like beautiful snake on measly rodent.

But final truth of Baseball transcend great player,
even Hawk, even Gibson, even Ruth and Gehrig.
Great Baseball team emerge from merging
of all, when all say, like great poet Robert Frost,
"Let me be the one to do what's to be done."
Let me chart pitch, let me move runner,
let me go in if needed. Base Ball communism,
communism America. Dmitri has come home.

If Freddie Greene

Dmitri would have face like happy platter,
and for most his life have given rhythm,
with Jo Jones and Walter Page,
and set great Count free to conduct,
by will through eyes with occasional plink,
play when and what Count wanted.

And once have had great privilege
of sing with Billie Holiday "Them
There Eyes," while she only mouthèd
words, with love, for that short time,
for me. And Pres stand back slanting
without jealousy, I think, of us or anything.

Dmitri's Agenda

> "'There are a hundred decisions he has to make every day, big decisions, with a lot riding on each one. So he'll give twenty of them to Karen to make.'"
>
> — Mark McKinnon, Presidential media advisor

What we can do for brave leaders,
even now at desks in hundred cities?
Make hard choice before breakfast,
they, continual brave and strong.

What we can do for brave leaders
who must preserve world from things
far worse than even death, many
far worse, far worse before breakfast?

Them you never see afraid and screaming,
them you never see crawl clutching
selves through blood and vomit, afraid
they might live, no, them you never see.

What we can do for such brave leaders,
continually brave and strong
in hundred cities before breakfast?
Must be something appropriate we can do.

Art Institute:
Picnic on the Grass

Dead, stiff, unmoving forms in pastel
palette stand on wall,
with dead dog try to bark
at dead boy sailboat in dead lake.

Seurat see perfect dream they sold
to middle class: that peace
mean no more motion,
no more anger, love, no more -

Just Eden in jar, with perfect seal
hermetic so that even molecule of air
stand still, and watch young wife
rest hand on young husband,

Never to clutch or claw or slap him,
For he will never grow borèd with
His perfect boring wife and child,
Perfectly fitted within their perfect clothes.

Dmitri saw today commercial on TV
in which this painting play great part.
And wonder at prophetic power
Of even most minor art.

Terrible Bug

This morning, Dmitri awaken to bug on shoulder,
as in James Bond movie, but not tarantula -
worse. This bug hairless, eyeless, armor plate
like rhinoceros but lustrous as low-rider.
Legs little complicated trick with stick,
antennae that move not more than rest of bug.
Bug just stand there, wait for Dmitri react.

And Dmitri cast back to time when friend Chris
show him indoor beehive, in which bee live life
behind glass, go out, come back through tube
through hole in apartment window Chris cut out.
Chris then had much enthusiastic for these
and tell Dmitri much - how they fly long, long way
from home, return unerring, all to feed queen.

Then Chris, who between wives, smack head
and say, "Bees good example God." How so?ask.
"Look all mad effort, astounding memory," Chris
say, "Dedication of worker, all to feed queen so
more worker born to do same." Bees worm
by bees, go in and out of hive, ones entering
furry in pollen, ones leaving clean to fly.

"My idea of God," Chris say, "is 'Smiling Jack
God. Now, Smiling Jack God not bad god,
but does lot of drug. So, make many invention
of variety kind. And," say Chris, "sometime
Smiling Jack God do too many drug,
and wake up in morning feel very bad !
And if He see you then - Here, wait -

have picture Smiling Jack God" -
Chris run out of kitchen, come back with book,
show Dmitri picture Franz Hals' "Mad Woman."
"There," say Chris, "that Smiling Jack God."

While Dmitri remember this, bug go on move,
up shoulder, onto pillowcase, onto sheet.
Dmitri leave him there, get up to see this day.

Alex

Alex comes knock at Dmitri's door
in middle of essential nothing doing.
Dmitri hear knock, reluctant answer,
and there is Alex from Konstantin.

See him off and on, in passing,
as is said, but always Dmitri respect
Alex, who is trained killer
and did much time in prisons,

because Alex always respect Dmitri,
and Dmitri well aware
that one thousand part of inch stand
between him and prison and murder.

Tonight Alex full empty.
Looking for what he don't know,
full of talking, story, quotation
from Bible and internet loon talk.

Brow knitted above sad eyes.
Dmitri, Alex say, I tell you how
this happen: then Alex speak
story of every one:

I fight to choose better over worse,
when I have any idea at all.

Cain and Abel

Behind hill, brothers fight
about nothing and everything.
Cain think, as Abel, that world
should belong to him.

The voice of god speak, saying,
Do not do this, my sons. Do not
fight each other, all women
will say the same to you.

But Cain say, Never mind, God,
I must be found correct, I must
have way. Abel, he always thought
he was better than anybody.

God keep saying, over and over,
"Oh, don't do that. Oh, don't do that.
Oh, don't do that." Hills surrounding
echo, Oh don't do that, Cain.

Cain say, "But Oh, God, cannot
you know how good it feel to take
life in hand and let it loose
with one quick slit across throat?"

And once question askèd, deed
is done, and Cain alone is left
to speak again with god, plead
case while Abel rot in sun.

Silent, god must consider now
why he did make such clever,
stupid creature in first place,
while Abel rot in sun.

Worrisome Condition

On TV was recently reveal new malady,
"the chronic, crippling fear of going
among groups of people." Name of malady:
"Social Anxiety Disorder." All his life
has Dmitri sufferèd in ignorance, until now.
Now, if he but buy pill - "Paxil," it is namèd -
he will be reconcile to herd, feel warm
and moo contented, like Elsie Borden Cow.

But is such anxiety "disorder"?
Do group of people truly moo
and crop, benevolent and peaceful?
Dmitri think not. In his experience,
Once group get much past five,
people turn to chicken. They do not amble,
rather strut and cower, they.
Turn into flightless, stupid, avian thug.

And when new chicken enter yard,
first question, only question:
can be peckèd? Or must let peck me?
New chicken best hope
not be perceivéd as peckable,
for, if is, all will fall upon him,
quick, coward beaks hack at his neck
once he is fallen, drive him into dust.

Are people cow? Chicken? No. People.
But people, Dmitri believe, not never meant
to herd up, covey up, flock up.
Not meant for group, these human.

Meant for pack, like wolf,
for pod, like whale. Therefore,

Dmitri's malady will remain uncurèd.
No Paxil. No pact with other chicken. No pax.

Blessing of Winter

When winter come, sailboat of rich vanish
from Belmont Harbor, and summer crowd
from beach, and then great lake return,
and by December, in good winter year,
lake start construction of escarpment,
wave on wave freezing to high, deep shelf,
sometime extend more than kilometre
from shore. And then can walk out upon,
sometime in early fog, until all white,
gray, until nothing of man remain,
not even Hancock Tower, city of men
left behind for world before and after.

Fathers

Of course Dmitri know America decadent,
full to spewing of capitalist grease,
and so no excess encounterèd when he
first come here did shock but one.

For in rack of record store, Goodwill,
of discount store and drug store
and little side street grocery store,
record, record, record. Records.

In Soviet Union, record only for rich.
Jazz Dmitri hear, only some Cossack idea
of some Georgian idea of jazz -
and still Dmitri love.

Then, in this new country, he does find
the famous cornucopia. The great machine
spill music as spill everything,
and what is precious is same

as day of week underpant or other fad
no longer faddish, consignèd
to bin and curb where only loser buy.
Ben Webster behind Tony Orlando.

What can poor Russian do
but take advantage of such madness?
And if great cornucopia machine
distinguish not between Shinola

and dead shit, cannot Dmitri

take his coin to market, find heart
of new country and take home
to Philco player found on Maxwell Street?

And thereon hear real voices
of America? Not Voice of America.
Voices. Sidney Bechet. Louis Armstrong.
Duke Ellington. Charles Mingus.

Thomas Waller. Bessie Smith. Gene
Sedric. Dick McDonough. Eddie Lang.
Each voice alive, unmistakeable,
full with individual heart, lung, soul, mind.

Dmitri would know voice of own father
if heard in crowd at soccer game.
Why take crazy Russian to recognize
voice of own sons, America?

Army

In training for Army, much madness
promulgated upon poor privates.
Dmitri recall a night of polishing
each handle of each sink with toilet paper,
until zinc shine like silver
for inspector who never come.

For many years, Dmitri have considered
obsession of his Army
with appearance. Conclusion:
army work for politician;
politician work for rich person;
rich person hate anything used before,

if cannot be bought and sold
at considerable profit, such as dead van Gogh.
Old plumbing, old cities, old animals -
phfffft. Old people - if they won't polish
up, let them go.

Old Man In Mirror

"The New Dodge: In a perfect world, everything would be different."
- Commercial message

This morning, shaving, Dmitri receive shock
of own visage, sudden that of father,
mother - uncle, who, in movie show in mind,
star as decrepit fart with mandolin.

How this happen to handsome young devil?
Dmitri have theory, as always.
Is conspiracy of capitalist inventor.
Do not laugh. Think:

First, electricity. Shortly, telephone.
Then talk go faster than talker can talk.
Then automobile. Then, flight.
Bodies hurlèd from here to there,

Like grains of sand in beanbag. Then,
radio, TV, computer, and thought
cannot keep up with transmitter.
Gigahertz. Ha. Miracle of progress

Bring all closer, world get smaller,
so conspirators insist, insist, insist.
But here their big lie,
for Faster not mean Closer.

People have own speed, not subject
to improvement by inventor.
People walk on two feet only, not
Gigafeet. Toast take time to toast.

And so, as all speed up around
and people scamper to keep up,
not get closer; get further part.
No talking during race. Save breath.

When uncle come to visit family,
and play on mandolin old song he learn
from many uncle passèd, sometime
Dmitri, family cry, brought close

to all, brought close to every all.
And uncle would touch tear from cheek
of one, beckon fingertip to tongue,
and smile as if taste fine wine.

But here in global village, such act as this
impossible, for uncle, niece,
father, daughter, all scatterèd,
flitting, fleeting, bouncing here to there,

Quick as electron in core of bomb,
Never at rest, never united.
And man who run all time alone....
No wonder he begin to look old

Memory

Young book buyer, lush and alive
as rosy peach, invite Dmitri
come home with her, continue talk
begun this afternoon in August.

Home in Winnetka, parent in Italy.
Ears perkèd, Dmitri close up shop,
hop in young goddess' Lexus chariot,
allow self to be transported.

Dmitri has seen this drive before,
but not this driver, whose roundness
pull his eyes, whose eager youngness
break and rebuild his hopeless heart.

Behind great fieldstone mansion, sip
chardonnay with goddess, within
vine-woven pergola - orange trumpetvine,
mauve Rose of Sharon, honeysuckle.

Most trumpet flowers now maturèd
to dangling, seedful pods, Dmitri
notice aloud, and air surpass
all perfume ever made by man.

In garden running down to shore of lake
stand Cosmos tall as grown girl,
their button centers visited
by bees. Ah, poetry, Dmitri.

As sun withdraw unseen behind,
and lavender of Russian sage intensify
in waning light, silence expand
as distance contract, and all seem right,

even appearance of family cat,
winding like melody between us two.
Then; then: this diabolic feline imp,
to give us full view, limp, crawl, mince

to frame of pergola, arch, quiver,
heave, deposit pool of liquid
yellow puke on bronze flagstone.
Too much like sourèd chardonnay.

Dmitri watch his goddess, experience
in this cat's moves, capture,
cradle, consider, and carry cat back
to house behind where Dmitri sit.

Return, arms free of accursèd cat,
knowledge in eyes that spell broken,
and evening end in Meow Mix treat
and drive back down Outer Drive.

Old memory, lush and alive
as featherèd skin of peach, sweet
as if fill mouth now, here, alone
with only riches spending save.

Bring It On

See Secretary of Defense in photo
at lunch with soldier in Iraq. Secretary
wear Air Cavalry hat. Perhaps got idea
from President when wear flight suit,
announce mission accomplish.

These aged boys like much dress up
in hero outfit, play soldier.
Imagine them in bathroom, late at night,
posing before mirror, make fast draw,
movie pistol sound at mirror. Pckshhhh.

So eager for war, these gentlemen
actors. When given chance, of course,
to go to actual war, then not so eager.
Why people of this country, or any,
fail to insist that great war leader

lead fight himself? Already have costume.
Already believe self untouchable,
untorturable, invulnerable.
Already believe reality what he say is.
Why people who believe such

cowardly fools not insist they act
like foolish cowards they are, lead charge
into valley death? Must be we
are more fools than fools in charge,
and greater cowards, too.

Conquerors

I, of course, had never been to war, but that was how I felt. Cooked to near death, as if my life in our culture had been some wretched and meaningless war in which the economy had become the only acceptable reality.
- Jim Harrison, The Beast That God Forgot to Invent

Living in country that has conquerèd
entire world, looking at faces
of conquerers on el, Dmitri ponder
memory of criminal cases

in former home. All those condemnèd
to die would stand in dock,
wait shivering for verdict
like chosen sheep from flock.

In country that has conquerèd
entire world, people at el stop,
headed for wonderful job,
look around for cop,

ingest drug of choice so can make
one more day in paradise.
All have their drug to take
to keep believe all rise.

All look as if condemnèd,
with eye unseeing other eye
or anything, anything, outside
lost confusion inside.

Pearl

My strange white cat who some bastard took front claws from lie on carpet across room. Often she take her front paws under chest to hide, ashamèd. But now she roll on back, fat and happy, seem as if nothing matter but comfort, in air lift defenseless paws, stretch toward sun not there, look like porn star, shameless in pleasure, give little moan of joy.

Pearl is name I give her. Pearl of great price, though cost Dmitri nothing but shots and pull sick teeth of poor girl. When enter house, keep to closet for month on month, then finally venture out. And other cat, all give Pearl berth, never challenge. And Pearl settle in, very slow, very slow,
to calmly center storm of Dmitri and his cats' life.

Pooled Black Rain

In narrow, deep shop beneath Van Buren el,
Dmitri sell old books. This his work,
this his joy. Even today in Russia,
Dmitri bet, books are first thing in home
that visitor led to. Was so, at least,
when long ago Dmitri was boy
and first allowed to open page,
read word set down by Pushkin,
Turgenev, Chekhov, Gogol, Tolstoy.

Quite then, those words in ink that stand
on page like pooled black rain
did seem like men who wrote Dmitri.
He could hear those great old men,
how they sweat blood to carve word
into paper, see tobacco in bushy beard,
hear heart near stop in sorrow at truth,
resume and gallop when laughter
found in same truth. Oh words on paper.

All sort come in from dark beneath el
to look at book in dark light of shop.
Old people, professor, writer, reader,
hunter after monetary gain. Dmitri sit
at desk deep back in shadow, watch.
He hunting, too. Hunt for self in customer,
look for telltale insignia of love.
Love not so much seen in eyes,
but in hands, as hands touch bindings, pages.

When young person enter store,
then does Dmitri alert, as when
fisher feel first tug of question
at bait far under lake. Is young person
lost? Does want cigarette, direction
to Gap Store, handout? Or does young person
seek for true connection to word?
Appearance give no clue at all.
Only insignia how book is touchèd.

And if Dmitri see young person sudden grasp,
gentle, swift, like bird dog duck,
one book, and open slow, and disappear
within, Dmitri smile. May rise from desk,
go out to question, may wait. Depend.
Watch young person face melt to real face,
as stupid self forgotten,
look up at long rows shelves,
contain so many hundred thousand year human.

Gospel According to Dmitri

In Beginning, laughter heard
at such idea as a Beginning.

Amidst laughter, a perfect world
(if not mind live and die) create itself.

It went on, went on,
living, dying,

until produce first people.
Then laughter become inaudible.

Amidst inaudible but increasing raucous
laughter, each generation did people attempt

suicide, in name of something
or other they construe as "victory."

Evidently, people believe life
best worship by means of murder.

No wonder people begin to hear
that laughter, not long before

the slow sea rose against them,
then over them, then was them.

In Beginning, waves laugh.

Art Institute: Francis Bacon's Elephant

Early in Dmitri days in USA, great excitement
come to Chicago: big traveling exhibit of work
by Francis Bacon, great English painter.
Dmitri never hear of, but, enticèd by last name,

go look at. Remember thinking Stalin
would be please at such purposeful wallow
in decadence: meat, meat, meat
is this Bacon theme, obsessive.

Great cattle, chests splay open to reveal
innards in which writhe more meat,
hangèd from meat hooks in shadow
lurid as inside mausoleum.

Portrait and portrait of people seen
as meat, waiting for meat hook,
waiting for knife. All look as if would
welcome blow of final mallet.

Dmitri wander slow among this charnel
place, in wonder that English fellow
know so much, refuse to lie about.
But then:

On short corner wall by portal
to next room, one painting huge and quiet
stop Dmitri in track of own dismal,
stop like good punch to forehead.

Never see this in book about Bacon,
so try to tell accurate. Imagine you stand
on West edge of African river,
deep forest at dawn all round, above.

Enough light in unseen sky to illuminate
shadow world of jungle. Across river,
great bull elephant, huge ears fan
to look for danger such as you,

emerge through brushy trees,
one paw tentative as pussy cat
testing breeze over edge of river.
Elephant look like he will step down,

step into river, swim.
Painting look like might have
happy ending. Here's peace for you,
and me, say Francis Bacon.

News

Saw boy once lash long pole
into crumple grey paper hornet nest.
That boy surprise very great.
Thought stick not only would destroy

nest, but kill all hornet in nest.
Thought hornet stupid and weak,
inferior species to great boy
who have such awesome stick to swing.

Their home destroyèd, hornet
fill air in mushroom cloud,
descend upon destroying boy,
sting, sting, sting until he crumple

to ground in shock as much
at number of opponent as at
venom. Did not expect, that boy,
his game be taken serious.

Body of boy lie twitching
until still. World go on, postman
deliver mail, nobody even notice
result of boy heroism.

Hornet immediate begin rebuild
grey cardboard home in eaves
of house where dead boy all life
had share with them breath.

Illusion

American poet cummings say
"Illusion better fate than truth."
How can Dmitri, dashèd hopes
Surrounding, disagree?

Yet does. Take, for illusion,
Perrault tale, "Cinderella."
When Prince fit shoe to foot,
How better ever will feel

That sudden elevated girl?
When Prince first find fault
With Cinderella cooking,
Will not truth intrude, gnawing?

Certain it will, as when Prince
sit trimming toenails
upon nuptial quilt,
and children puke, et cetera.

Then will begin great game:
to remember what Prince
and Cinderella saw
one minute before midnight.

No Einstein

"The whole affair is a matter of indifference to me, as is all the commotion, and the opinion of each and every human being."
- Albert Einstein to Max Bohr

"...for all his kindness, sociability and love of humanity, he was nevertheless detached from his environment and the human beings included in it." - Einstein according to Max Bohr, his friend

When people want to say guy not too smart,
say often, "He no Einstein." Epitome
of wisdom, Einstein. J-Lo of wisdom.
Dmitri wonder. Dmitri wonder.

A man indifferent to opinion
each and every human being.
But world know many such - so many,
even have created name for type.

"Sociopath," so such are callèd, no?
Who care not for other feeling, other love or fear,
because have none of own, and so believe
that all just acting, all other empty as they?

To feed such emptiness no food suffice.
And so no victory, no perfect crime,
no nothing, short of eat whole universe
suffice. Oh yes, world know many such.

This fountainhead modern wisdom, Einstein,
spend all last years in search for unified field,
for One Big Answer. This man who fled Nazis
to seek eternal-year Reich for Physics.

Detach from his environment, yes. Living,
if want to call it that, in freedom, if want to
call it that, of his big brain. Dmitri can show
you any number such down in South Wabash bar.

Very free, these, have not notice environment
since Jesus pup. Can show more such
any night on television, full only of bile
and disappoint with world that outside head.

Never notice perfume of world,
flower that bloom and turn to shit,
notice only hollow little click
that thought make striking other thought.

If by fruit, as Jesus say, can know,
then taste such fruit as grow at Chernobyl,
Bopal, Hiroshima. Our great teacher
have barely begun lesson.

Intelligent Design. Good Question.

Dmitri have number of experience of universe,
including death by pneumonia when see recede
below him continents of world as ride on back
of some great bird and marvel at world beauty.

Even, once, when under influence of contollèd
substance which of course not recommend
to youth of world, Dmitri meet Jesus in person,
in place among stars. Was friendly, Jesus.

None such experience have fed, can feed
one cat Dmitri harbor, one wino found
in entryway, slump like bag of clothing
left at back door of Goodwill, never mind rain.

No. Experience of universe belonging
to Dmitri or any other human, including astronaut,
too limited to give possessor right to opinion.
Tick think dog universe, and may be right.

President of this country on this earth in this
universe think world so complicated that
must have been made by some engineer
who also like to forgive killer who no longer drink.

Dmitri cannot argue. Such engineer could also
have make shark or supernova, and have
jerk from shark jaw Hitler on way to gullet,
or from big explosion Mother Teresa.

If some power right name God do run this show,

as Dmitri run apartment and bookstore,
then should all ask, as dust or ant or wasp
would if could, why me, why me, why me?

Of course, in end, all do.

Invitation to Wedding

Sotto voce, a male guest standing at the fringe of the wedding ceremony says out of the corner of his mouth to a guy standing next to him, "I don't bother with all this. I simply find a woman who hates me, and I give her a house."

- Kurt Vonnegut, Timequake

Young customer come in, invite
Dmitri to her wedding. Why not?
Though, from experience, Dmitri quail
at thought of what will befall.

Same time, Dmitri think, Why not?
Perhaps will be there bridesmaid
befuddlèd by occasion.
Yes: into passion for old man.

There is it. Hope. Hope
will drive this young woman
into arms, then house, then life
of some young man, and chances

are that he and she will end
in hate or ugly sadness with children.
Dmitri hope not.
Dmitri know odds.

Dmitri know this, also: pay
for all choices, and sometime,
rarely, get what pay for.
Dmitri will be guest at wedding.

Not So Good Friday

In bar so deep from front to back
that back not visible from Wabash
entrance, Dmitri sometime drink,
when arms of home fail to beckon.

Tonight, Good Friday, such a night,
and there Dmitri sit, head over drink
between elbows on walnut bar,
next to old floozie with mad eyes.

"You!" she say, sudden. "You."
Dmitri, assuming she speak to dead,
continue to consider content of glass.
Then louder and in ear, "YOU!"

So must turn on stool and look.
"Yes, mademoiselle. Your pleasure?"
respond, with dread in vein
at prospect of this interchange.

"I always," say crone, and stop.
Dmitri wait, polite. "I always,"
say crone again, "hate hour
between one and three this day."

Time now, well beyond midnight.
"Why so?" think best inquire.
Perhaps will be beginning joke,
though not much hope of this.

"Because," say raisin mouth, "because
this was the time they beat Jesus -
from one to three this afternoon."
Lips purse to emphasize nod.

"Da," I say. She seem satisfièd,
turn away toward mirror. Seem
satisfièd by what she see there,
too, and small smile form as eyes close.

Da. They beat Jesus between
one and three. Then. Now.
Also, between midnight and one,
also between three and midnight.

Also in Jerusalem, in Beirut,
Nairobi and Tangier, Dar-es-Salaam,
Calcutta and Beijing, Glasgow,
Vladivostok, Nuremberg, Chicago -

How many city have we made?
None: no city where Jesus
has escapèd knout. Writhe
like spearèd snake, my friend -

already you know only way out.

Tar

Look up at mighty struts
supporting el. Coated with
coal dust, oil, sputum
of all years since birth.

These spars like teeth
of old men, revealèd
by sad laughter
in smoky taverns.

Sad, ugly, stain
by million experience,
upright, crooked, strong.
Perhaps these stain

of years make stronger
than shining teeth of those
who ride above,
secure in modern dentistry.

Critical Failure

Long ago in letter,
Dmitri try to tell Tendryakov
his day ended. Nobody
interested anymore in people.

Tendryakov refuse to listen,
go on writing about poor people.
About, for instance, poor girl
who tend pig for bureaucrat.

"Vladimir," I tell him, "Nobody
in America care about nobody
who tend pig!" "How not?"
Vladimir respond; "do they not

eat ham?" "Of course do," respond,
"but think ham come from supermart."
"I tell them otherwise,"   say Vladimir.
"Good luck," I say.

Faith in America

Dmitri once see old black white movie
on old black white TV in apartment
on Astor Place. Girl who live there
passèd out before great lover
have chance demonstrate prowess.

Before pass out, had drag by arm
Dmitri to bay window, direct him
to look down through leafless elm
at actual cobblestone street, black
from Chicago Fire, still here, now,
to shine blacker yet in sleet and rain.
Quite far from here, she say, did
famous cow kick over famous lamp,
burn most of city down. Now only
these cobblestone remain.

Old black white movie name
Steel Helmet. Told of platoon
in Korea War, led by sergeant
play by great actor Neville Brand.
Platoon have no luck but bad,
and at end, sergeant pinnèd down
in shack with dying North Korean,
knowing both to die before long
when shack overrun by crazy gooks.

Sergeant look out one dirty window

at dawn early light, hear death rattle
in gook throat, say, "Buddy -
you got religion?" North Korean soldier
strangle, "Buddhist."

Then sergeant slide arm beneath
dying enemy head, lift gentle, say
"Buddha bless you, then."
And enemy die in such cradle. And then,
outside in unseen grey morning,
hear enemy tank and troop approach.
End of movie.

Make Dmitri cry. This was America
Dmitri thought he come to, where
people respect other people,
in spite difference, enmity, fight.
In spite color of mere skin,
country of parent, name of god.

Here in apartment of some American
cherishèd daughter, who only know
what guidebook say of own street,
who cannot hold liquor,
Dmitri rise from TV stupor, turn off tube,
dumb tear run out of eye,
and stumble back to window,
throw up lower pane,
sing with voice of Chaliapin
first American song ever learn:

Say is only paper moon
Sail over cardboard sea
But would not be make believe
If you believe in me?

Silence

When late Spring afternoon
grow sudden purple,
and windows darken as if bruisèd by night,
and leaves of trees hang languid,
glow greener as dark get darker yet,
Dmitri rise from kitchen table,
turn off Gene Ammons in mid lope,
and make way down three flights
to stoop, where stand awaiting
holy wrath of coming storm.

One time in such storm,
great arrow of lightning
did strike light pole, maybe one yard
from where Dmitri put one foot down.
Great white phosphorous glare,
then gigantic sizzle, as of whole world's
bacon thrown in one pan, then,
for maybe one second that seem stretchèd
out of time, pure silence
make bubble, in which Dmitri stand.

You do not know silence.
No little birds, no slamming doors,
no distant music bad or good,
no whish of tires, random people yak
from radio or tv, no sound
from own belly or lung
or stupid tape in head -
silence. As Buddha hear, perhaps,
beneath the Bodi tree.

Pure being, all meaning erasèd,

being in place we start and end.

And then and then and then:
Explosion
as if Dmitri inside bomb,
and then
new silence of deaf, of shock.

After time resume, Dmitri look around
expecting sights of war.
But no windows lie in splinters,
no walls in chunks on sidewalk.
All as was, cop car rounding corner,
old woman white toy poodle
crapping by edge of curb.

Standing on stoop, Dmitri remember,
run down steps into first staggering
drops of rain,
hoping to hear silence once more.

Cells

In cell, of which Dmitri do not like to think,
sit men Dmitri do not know, but meet on daily basis
when their brother drink in tavern
on Clark or Ogden Street.

All stories same: he is good guy, brother -
took care of me, won race, won fight, won prize. Took
one wrong step, and now our poor mother every night
sit home emptying her eyes.

Dmitri do not know how to talk to these relative, who
have come up street from Mass to drink with him,
and when he speak, eyes freeze at talk that in this
country might have "class."

Kiss him goodbye, he will not return to you.
Worst you ever imagine: that is true.

Children

Into my bookshop come children,
though not look like, with sad, pale face
already line in black around scimitar
line of disappointment.

Come in, most, for place to go
no cop nor fiend nor parent find them -
for brief rest. Then leave, into street
where still think life with capital "L" live.

Of course they are misled. Life
in streets is jungle.
Is desert. Life does not live
in this city or other. Live in water,

in dirt, fly through top of tree
and burrow through grass.
No life can eat concrete,
nor breathe electric dot.

These children who come in,
send away with silent hope
that they survive, and little
hope they will, in this desert.

They will walk out Dmitri door
and there to meet them will be
Angel of Death dressed up
in sexiest outfit Madonna ever dream.

Everything Modern

Enjoy watching young girl
think selves hot stuff
prance twitching melons,
midriff bare to all,
no doubt in mind that have
invented stylish come-on,

and boyfriend, slack face
bereft of hair, terrible decade
of goatee and giant pants forgotten.
(Good thing, too. Goatee
make mock of many callow sport.)

Both will wake one morning
to not so easy day to face,
kids wearing clothes they wore
when world was theirs.

Everything modern
until not.

Women Laughing in My House

Last time Dmitri hear real laughing in house
when friend Alexei die. Many woman, then,
at church, then over to Dmitri place, where
had competed to make good food for death.

Death of friend great occasion for phony.
All present at funeral display grief and wonder
upon physiognomy, while check watch
and think about where next get what want.

Dmitri talk with grievers for long while,
then escape to kitchen, where find grieving widow
and old Dmitri girlfriend double over selves,
laughing. Drunk, to be sure, but real laughing.

"What in Name of Blessed Savior," ask Dmitri,
"have come upon such woman as you?"
As Dmitri knew, such remark prompt
hysteria, which will lead to real crying.

Women think men know nothing.
Have good reason.
Dmitri, loving women for near 60 year now,
grateful for only advantage left.

Would happy share his great wisdom
with Alexei, were he not dead.
He would not listen dead more
than ever he did alive.

Precedent

"Genetics is all about who's boss. And we always want to be the boss."
- Mary Rogan, "Penninger"

Have just read best news
imaginable: God has been found.
Was hiding all along
in thymus gland.

Now Austrian scientist
working for Canadian millionaire
has track God down,
and God is finally cornerèd.

Now can stand in dock, God,
who put contract on so many
innocent babies born to war
and born to poorness.

Now! Who is God Almighty
now, eh? We! Us!
Human Almighty at last!
Dmitri would praise new God,

but modesty forbid.
Instead, will wait to see
how new God comport self.
Precedent not encouraging.

Neighbors

...and it is difficult to resent with proper and durable indignation the physical or mental anguish of another organism, even if that organism is one's own father.
  - Joseph Conrad, Nostromo

A small man who collected stamps
live next door, until the day
the men arrive in hollow boot
and thunder knock and in handcuff
took him away, already broken.

Great poet Ahkhmatova sought
for years after her son,
disappeared into system
of Soviet Justice. She did
never find neither.

Here in land of free,
neighbor disappear
quite prompt and frequent,
guilty of wrong skin or poverty or weakness,
already broken.

As in original country, in this one
no one speak of vanish neighbors.

And so no one speak.

Some Work for Living

Neighbors in apartment across hall
young lawyers, and at first
hold many parties with drink,
loud rock of college days,
much emphatic and sincerity
shouting after midnight, sometime
naked people run in hall,
sad murmur of voice or two at dawn.
Dmitri not good sleeper anyway,
never complain. Sit up with drink
in hand and lamplight, Gogol
or other funny book in lap.
Own youth absent gaiety,
enjoy own youth by proxy,
like capitalist, as if get to own
what owners vote to buy.

As years continue, parties wane,
young lawyers grow black furrows
over bridge of new eyeglasses.
Perhaps have choose wrong specialty,
poor criminals instead of rich.
Have no longer glow when meet
at stairway door. But still attorneys,
so we speak in careful polite.
Tonight, Yuri, Alex, Sandra, other women,
other friend all come together here,
party ensue, much song and dance of sort,
sound of object breaking, talk,
laugh, talk, laugh. Big knock on door.
Is neighbor lawyer lady, pissed.
"Some people work for living," say.
"Some people live," say. Close door gentle.

Stem Cell

On radio, TV, without surcease for days,
people talk about stem cell.
Question: should human create life
to kill in order to prolong or save human?

This would be deep question indeed,
if, for example, askèd by chimpanzee.
Should human further advance ability
to live life wiping out all other?

Should human further advance ability
to live life of contempt for us chimps?
Wish I to see my captor prevail
outside these bars he put around us?

Wish I to see this human Goliath
enlarge himself further so his feet
may more convenient crush
my former forest as he suck all remaining air?

Chimp Dmitri see put finger to
sparse hair chin, ask why human
should continue, given record,
to enjoy further stay of execution.

Days of Infamy

And on that day when some great man with stick
smash from air last final passenger pigeon,
And on that day when some great man with pen
sign to Chief Joseph agreement that he spat upon
before the eyes in back of that Chief's head,
And on that day first slave stood chainèd
on platform, and some man with butt of whip
his black rib prod, assuring quality
of product before purchase,
And on that day some men invisible,
so high they flew, flattened city Nagasaki,
left shadow people lie in shadow trees,
And on that day some FBI with badge
had word with some employer, and some man
lose livelihood, then family, then hope, then life,
And on that day Columbia River Dam complete,
and River begin to lose life,
And on that day in Chile when Allende die,
in Vietnam when Dragon Lady choke on blood,
when boys too young to drink string ears to send
home pickled in jar for souvenir -
Was terror present?

And on that day when poor man,
sick of poorness, murder wife and kids
as TV retail Lifestyle Rich and Famous,
And on that day when radio personality
scream Penalty of Death for Druggies,
loaded on legal speed and hatred,
And on that day when newspaper editor with pen

attempt to delete Spotted Owl, and, not content,
all those who care for ought but dollar,
And on that day when teacher quit,
musician quit, nurse, grocer, bookseller quit,
and line up supplicant to computer king,
And on that day when children, ring in eyelid,
lie in motel injecting last of hope,

And on that day when Presidential mouthpiece,
hologram of hologram, announce free speech
most inappropriate to present time, and every
corporation sprout flag from out its anus,
and dead not cold before become logo -
Is terror present?

Czeslaw Milosz, who live through Nazis, then   through
my people, said this of man innocent of terror:
"He cannot believe that one day
a rider may appear
on a street he knows well,
where cats sleep and children play,
and start catching passersby with his lasso."

The rider has arrive.

Geese

December and I saw geese
walking out on Lake Michigan
resembling aldermen

striding forward
over slippery sidewalks
toward City Hall,

chins tucked to show
irreproachable dignity
in spite ice.

Dogs

Neighbor up hall, Carol, ask me,
"Dmitri, can take care of dogs
while I away in New York City?"
How could Dmitri deny her this chance
to visit Big Apple, where all TV
originate? Da, Da, Da, Dmitri say.

First day, take dogs to park
according instruction, one on leash,
one without because trainèd.
Leashed one, Missy; free one, Fred.
Fred seem happy,
Missy, not so happy.

Dmitri, thinking self master of at least
dog fate, if no other,
release Missy, and all go well, for while,
until in distance appear human shadow,
rapidly turn into female jogger,
and Missy see, then Fred.

Like Furies off they tear, and jogger,
before she quite aware,
beset at heels by these two curs,
yap, snap, yap yap yap.
As crazy stranger run toward her,
screaming Russian curses.

Was not how she envisionèd jog,
nor what Dmitri hoped of peaceful stroll.
Sudden screams and blood

from puncture heel, chaos in microwave
time - no, no, this was not program.
Was buff for Success, was make easy money

going to park with nice doggies.
Now dust and claws and racing heart
and, after dogs quell, and Missy back
on leash, then full dose of humiliation
for Dmitri from young jogger -
in NPR style, invoking many new principle

of behavior before now unheard of.
All time taking this, Dmitri aware that
prosecutor nipples quite extraordinarily large
beneath her sweaty t-shirt.
After profuse apology, mollified
yuppiette resume her jog, Dmitri his stroll
with dogs, now happy panting,
numbers increasèd by one.

Art Institute: Caillebotte

"Honeywood was a robot, a set of reactions, a creature ruled entirely by prejudice and a mass of contradictory impulses and inhibitions, which he called his opinions, and thought of as his character."
                      - Joyce Cary, The African Witch

    Big painting, nearly size of life, confront
    with perfect Parisien pair, un bon vivant
    under beaver bowler hold umbrella
    above most precious curls of m'amselle

    whose tender pink cheeks reflect
    tears in air, rain in halo hair,
    tears to come, though this
    she do not know at all,

    though all around gleam wet
    as if sky cried at seeing such
    happy young creature
    about to be eaten by such

    contented, fat, fatuous, empty
    young man of sort who own
    Parisien street upon which
    now, she walk so happy

    beneath protecting shield
    held by this victor man with mustache,
    chest bursting vest,
    almost size of life.

May Day

On May Day in Grant Park,
no parade, no demonstration,
only Dmitri walking on path
where cops club people in 1968.

Astonishing how many colors
green may manifest
in youthful leaves.
Painters have name them all.

Not painter, Dmitri still see
how one tree, green,
set off the one beside it,
also green, as lemon

set off lime, as fuse
ignite bomb,
as hope set off
hope each Spring.

Two mounted cops sit
horses as Dmitri pass,
ironically salute with nightsticks.

Dmitri smile pretty.

Hockey Jazz

When trumpet, clarinet, trombone
weave like great hockey forward line
through time on slippery ice,

arrive by twist and turn at mouth of goal,
pass puck from stick to stick,
lead note from horn to horn,

and goal too good to score,
cadence too sweet to end -
Then. Then

Dmitri believe human
already here, and
yet may be born.

Salvation of America

Dmitri read one time of greatest flock crows
recorded, in western state of Oregon,
tens thousands crows. If all fly at once,

your sky not disappear. Turn black,
as if Satan move in to stay.
No wonder people fear.

Put ad in papers, Come Kill Crows,
oh, help us, please.
Help come. Quite soon,

flock sanitize,
survivor disperse.
Now only earth black.

Those Savèd From All Sin

As Russian, can scarcely deny experience
of corruption. Of language, by elimination
of certain word, replacèd by official new.
George Orwell describe process perfect,

and how may lead to terribleness
that cannot be seen, therefore not questionéd.
Dmitri has notice that old word "honor"
seem to have disappearèd quite entire.

Tonight on news, successful pharmacist
admit diluting drug of his cancer patient.
Though multimillionaire, had cash flow
problem, and had promisèd his Church

big donation. Answer present self:
screw dying, too helpless to notice.
"Honor" not word in this man mind.
Have other formula close ready to grasp.

Don't let right hand know what left hand
do when pluck out neighbor eye.
Is right there in Bible : Word of God.
And so they did. And so they do.

Bumper Sticker

See many bumper sticker that cleverly proclaim
God is woman. Imagine all who drive vehicle
so adornèd listening to Public Radio,
East Coast voice that tell what best people think today.

Still, bumper sticker stick in craw of mind.
If God woman, and if Dmitri woman,
would Dmitri lose female self in hosanna
for grand design of female deity?

Dmitri would spend one quarter life
feeling as if bad seafood ripped at guts,
belly pushing belt and nipples at too tight shirt,
and no one to blame but dear Mother God.

Then, for relief, would bleed out minerals
and eggs, all in order to await miracle
of pregnancy, leading to agony known only
to such men as die of serious torture,

and no one to blame but dear Mother God
when little miracle become thirteen and turn
and rend like weasel self and me,
run off with greasy-hair young swine

who will her leave in lurch with baby own,
to bring home to mama. Circle of life.
By now, good chance papa long gone
to find new baby for himself.

Believe Dmitri would do as woman do,
and did, and will do: create God of better world,
where all fall easily and just,

blame foreign devil for all wrong here on earth.

And foreign devil, weary of bearing weight
of unremediable blame, would throw up hands,
say, If devil you say and feel I am,
get ready for more of same and more than that.

Dmitri often think that Jew get almost there,
stop one step short. Jahweh best name for God,
say we cannot call name. No God better.
Leave man, woman with selves to blame.

American Movie

Happy end always set scene:
The Family together with the pie,
soft and gaping. Old Uncle and Grandpa
make comic comment, junior laugh.

But then, villain arrive through
french door, twirling gun and mustache,
so villainhood not missèd.
Insert gun in granny gum,

say, "Do this, or I do this."
Little Cousin Susie make run
at gun in villain hand, he slap
her silly, laugh, and wait.

Now there is no question
this is Evil man, and Father hold
his breath and wait until he turn
to sneer at Granny, and attack,

fly like eagle over living room
to pinion Evil one to floor,
grab gun, grab throat, and after
some kicking, rise somewhat abashèd,

Say, "Look, darlings, I have vanquish
foe. Look: here in my very hand,
his Evil throat, complete with
veins, thorax, blood."

Wife, daughter, mother, all turn
away, and great American hero left,
once again, with blood on hand
and no one to applaud.

Look down at guts between fingers,
like chef at feast no one has come to,
and cannot find cloth
with which to wipe fingers clean.

Want to know what Dmitri
think, want doubloon
from treasure Dmitri capture
from long experience?

Dmitri think is always war.

Between what all imagine
when pronounce word "humane,"
and what Nelson Algren once describe
as "wildest beast that still roams free,"

war must continue forever.
War within. War without.

And to that beast so wild within,
All act of resistance, any act
of resistance, any -
we must cherish. We must emulate.

Eric Nesterenko

Through pal Andrei, Dmitri once meet
Eric Nesterenko, great right wing
of Chicago's Blackhawks,
at party of sorts Andrei make after game
against Canadians, which Chicago,
of course, lose by number goals.

Andrei have house in suburbs
with long, low wreck room underneath,
and Nesterenko enter angry,
very tall man, nearly have to stoop
to get to bar, where he refuse glass,
clutch whisky bottle in one hand,

upend. Throat gurgle for some time.
Throat long, like heron's,
and adam's apple bob rhythmic.
Set bottle down most gently
upon Andrei's bar, announce
in high voice following wisdom:

"Love," say Nesterenko. "Love,
gentlemen - and any ladies present -
Love is a quivering of the gonads."
Then once again grasp and upend
bottle, and once more adam's apple
bob as James Brown scream in background.

Some hour or two before this moment,
Dmitri had watched this man
skate up right boards with puck,
pass behind back across ice to great center

Latvia Stan Mikita, elbow defenseman
out of way, skate in toward goal

and take Mikita's pass between legs,
fake right, fake left, shoot high right,
and score one solitary goal for team.
And in those seconds, hockey become
what it begin from: game for kids
on frozen pond with no one watching.

Later in same evening, while Alexei
prompting girls to take tits in hands,
and music too loud to be music,
Dmitri approach Nesterenko.
Cadaver face narrow as blade,
eyes sad as any Russian's,

Nesterenko put hand into Dmitri's,
bow slightly, nod, and look into eyes.
No words. But Dmitri hear words
from Nesterenko silence. These
words Dmitri hear: "The strong
can be kind." Dmitri never forget.

Dry Spring

Little snow this winter for Chicago,
and now so little rain through April, May
that hardiest of tree display bare sticks
to reach as prayer to deaf ear sky.

All great leader agree that worrièd
none should be, that climate is thing
of mystery, and as another chunk of
polar ice cap capsize into sea,

that progress must progress, and will.
Dmitri, drunk, read headline inside eye
and would entire despair but for
few drops rain he find on windowsill,

clean spot like cancer of life in soot.
Notice, leaning suicidal out
after yet other Cub loss,
that bare fingers bear hint buds.

Missy and Fred

Oh, friend Dmitri, neighbor call,
can take my doggies over weekend
Christmas while I visit Brad and family?
How could Dmitri not?

Dmitri sit beneath window looking out
at black snow on street,
Fred panting quiet in his paws,
Missy brown weight in lap.

How can Dmitri tell these two dog
that Christmas is story for them?
Heave Missy up from lap, call
Fred to kitchen, give biscuit to all.

Then resume seat at window,
imagine great joy for Fred &Missy
owner, wrappèd in arms of friend
who love her dear in cold down.

Fred! Dmitri say; Missy! Come!
Dogs rousèd, all make pilgrimage
to lake shore, watch wave
arrive as other wave depart.

Kill Dmitri

In coffee shop beneath el,
in always permanent shadow,
old people come to talk,

but only to each other.
By need for coffee, Dmitri
one time driven to this place,

and as he enter, elder eyes
slash and dismiss him,
old folded lips curl scorn

for man who wear foreign cap
and hips still move.
Or maybe just for stranger.

Quickly, in cooked egg,
burnt coffee, wet wool atmosphere,
old people resume their talk.

Then, then what a litany commence
of ache and pain and hemorrhoid,
of Doctor Say and Doctor Say Not.

Oh did hear you how Charlie fell
from ladder, stupid Charlie,
what he was thinking, get on ladder?

Compete, they, to count infirmity
like rosary bead. Trade doctor name
like baseball card.

I tell you this:
First time you hear him mention
own state of health, kill Dmitri.

Health not broken parts.
Health wholeness of resolve
to live until killèd.

Must Be Old, Dmitri

In still, late autumn afternoon,
miraculous devoid of even breeze,
Dmitri recline on Grant Park bench,
examine drift of fallen leaf on pathway,
watch as light take less, less color
from dying leaf on tree and bush and grass.

Must be old, Dmitri, to find such joy
in waning season, in such moment
of no motion, soundless slow drama
of one moment merging into next,
pointless, inexorable, without word.

Now, sudden, birds begin announce
advent of nightfall, time return
to nest, and slightest gust
cross over park, make quiver

sumac leaves remaining on their boughs
as skin tremble to touch of lover,
as water quiver from invisible fish.

Dmitri must be old to feel such joy
to share such common life,

let alone to cry, "Too much! Too much!"

www.ingramcontent.com/pod-product-compliance
Lightning Source LLC
Chambersburg PA
CBHW031206090426
42736CB00009B/806